food items is rarely a problem, given the right species. A growing number of pet shops can give sound advice on the correct management of snakes in captivity, but there still is considerable room for further advancement in this area.

A sure sign of the success of the hobby is the great number of species now being captive-bred. Not so many years ago even zoos struggled to breed almost any species of snake. Snake breeding continues to be a rewarding challenge to the interested breeder.

The newcomer to snake keeping must not purchase any of the venomous species, and there also are many non-venomous species that should not be acquired by the novice. This book discusses mainly those species considered suitable for keeping in the average home. Mention is made of species unsuitable for beginners in order that the work be reasonably comprehensive. These species should be purchased only when a sound knowledge of general snake husbandry and the solemn responsibilities of snake owning have developed.

Psammophis jallae (**Rhodesian Sand Snake**). Occurring in southern Africa and parts of Asia, this rear-fanged species inhabits extremely dry regions and is almost never seen for sale in the pet trade. ◂

Phimophis guerini (**Speckled Ground Racer**). Rarely growing over 90 cm/36 in, this resident of Brazil southward to Argentina feeds mainly on lizards and needs to be kept in a very dry terrarium. ◂

Artwork depicting two vipers. ◂

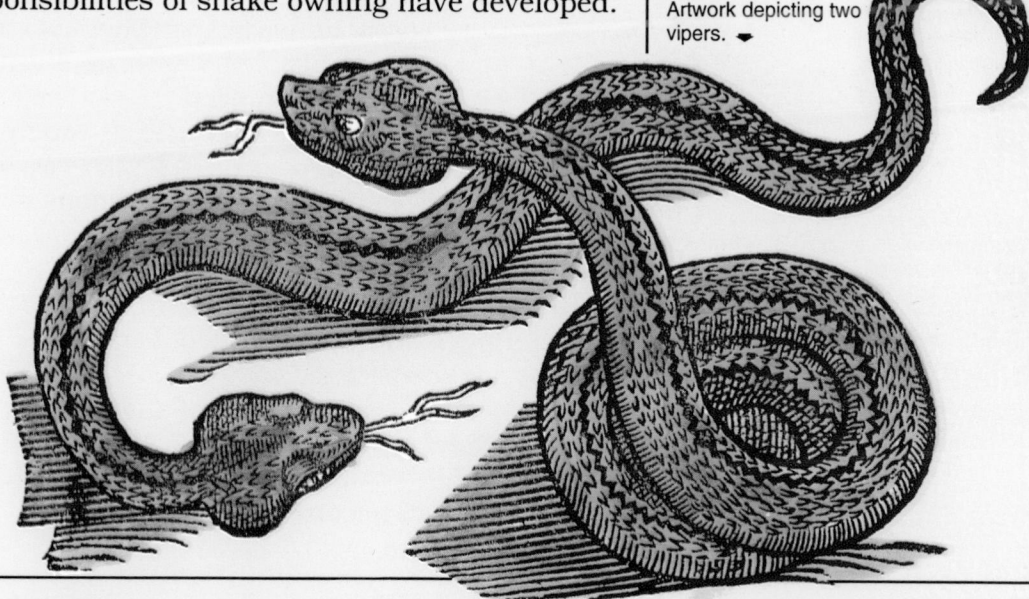

3

Lampropeltis triangulum (**Milk Snake**). Among the most commonly kept snakes are the Milk Snakes. There are many subspecies in this somewhat confusing group. Most of them make excellent captives and some are commercially bred in large numbers. ◆

Crotalus durissus (**Neotropical Rattlesnake**). A strikingly attractive snake, this and all other "rattlers" make very poor pets because they are simply too dangerous to keep in the home. Even the most advanced keepers should avoid poisonous species. ◆

This aspect of responsibility cannot be over-stressed. The average person has a fear of snakes, hence it is totally irresponsible for any snake owner to show off a snake in a frightening manner. Snakes are struggling to shrug off an unsavory reputation. Each snake enthusiast should be an ambassador in the attempt to re-educate the public.

The Pet Snake

Planning

Give careful thought to the matter of buying a snake before you do it. Be sure to discuss it with the rest of your family. The person with no previous snake experience is advised to restrict the selection to those species that generally are easier to keep in captivity and are not venomous. The experience gained from your first snake later can be applied to the more exotic species. Avoid large snakes. They require more costly housing and there also may be more problems associated with their general upkeep.

The best advice is to read as much as you can about the species in which you are interested, then visit a variety of pet shops to ascertain its availability. Join a local herpetological society and attend regular meetings. Question members about the characteristics and potential problems of different snake species.

Also, check the accessibility of snake foods in your area. Seek a veterinarian who has experience with snakes. Only once all the preliminaries are accomplished is it time to acquire the snake.

Pituophis sayi (**Bullsnake**). Very common in the herpetological hobby, Bullsnakes are usually reasonably priced and captive-bred specimens do remarkably well in captivity. They are hardy, long-lived, and very willing to eat. ☛

Where To Buy

The best and most obvious place for a purchase is a pet shop. Some do not stock reptiles, but many do. It is best to deal with a store that keeps a number of species in stock. This suggests that the shop does a healthy trade in snakes, therefore it has sales people experienced with snakes. It is also important that the store is clean, neat, and well stocked. The cages must be well kept. Select a pet shop with a good reputation. This is the shop you will return to for sound advice and the necessary supplies. It always pays off in the long run to purchase from a good source, even if it means paying a little more for your snake. There are no bargains when it comes to a healthy pet.

Lampropeltis triangulum (**Milk Snake**). Geographically, Milk Snakes are very widespread, occurring as far south as Ecuador and as far north as southern Quebec. ☛

Health

Boa constrictor (**Hog Island Boa**). One of the lesser-known Boa Constrictor varieties, this snake has earned notoriety for its unpredictable temperament. Its captive care is similar to that of other Boa Constrictors. ➤

The eyes of a snake must be clear. A healthy snake has a smooth, supple body, with no signs of parasites, bites, or swellings apparent at any point along its length. If it has recently shed its skin, there should be no bits of skin adhering here and there to suggest that its health is not as it should be.

Snakes are affected by most of the conditions that afflict other animals. Lack of a balanced diet, worm infestations, and other ailments show themselves in a snake that is listless, lacking good form, and with eyes that are less than bright. If the color of the snake is washed-out or faded compared to others of the species, make another selection.

Age and Sex

It is preferable to purchase a young snake. You will have it as a pet for that much longer. Also, a young snake adjusts more easily to a captive environment and a change in diet. However, young specimens may be more difficult to sex.

Helicops sp. (**keelback snake**). Native to South America, this attractive fish-eater is not often seen in the pet hobby. Specimens, however, are said to be fairly hardy and can be kept in a paludarium (half-land, half-water setup). ➤

If possible, buy captive-bred specimens. You get a healthier snake and do not put pressure on already stressed wild populations. Captive-bred snakes may be a bit more expensive, but young specimens are more readily adaptable to captivity than wild-caught specimens. Many snakes are now captive-bred.

If you plan to keep more than one snake, purchase two females or a male and a female. Animals introduced at a young age have a better chance of adjusting to one another. Obtain

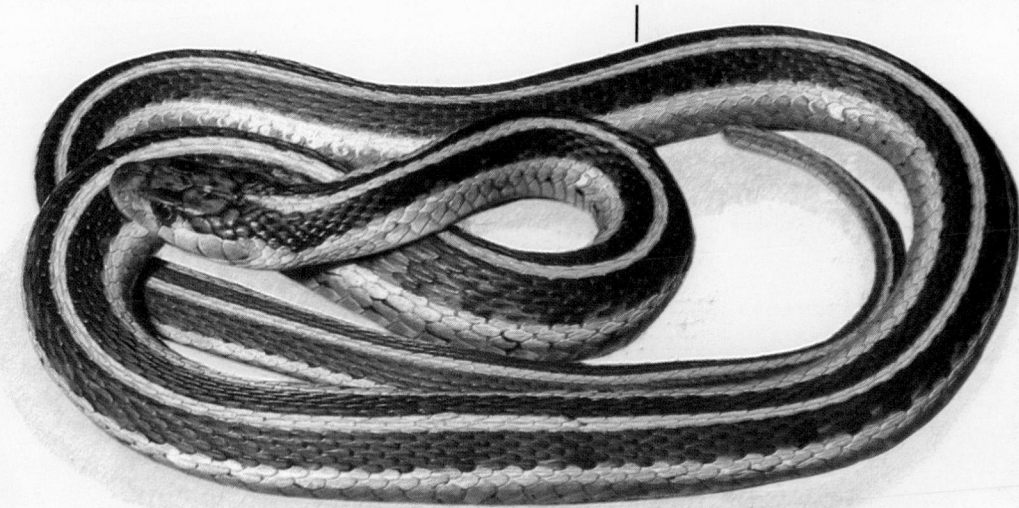

Thamnophis sirtalis infernalis (**California Red-sided Garter Snake**). A most remarkable little snake: females have been known to give birth to over 70 young! Most specimens are very bold and will bite when grabbed. ▲

Lampropeltis triangulum andesiana (**Andean Milk Snake**). The Andean Milk Snake is found exclusively in the Andes Mountains in Colombia. Note the heavy black mottling on the snake's "cheeks." This is one subspecies not likely to be seen in the hobby anytime soon.
▼

snakes of about the same size to minimize the chance of one devouring the other.

Transporting Home

Before bringing the snake home, find out what it was being fed. Ask when it last fed and how often it ate. Take note of the temperature. Snakes have preferred temperature ranges. These can differ in the same species if that species has a wide range of distribution. The idea is to minimize the stress of the transition as much as possible.

Your newly purchased snake should be carried home in a suitable container. In the case of a small snake, a cardboard, wooden, or plastic box with a lid pierced with holes will suffice. Paper or moss placed inside will prevent the snake from being tossed about.

A larger snake should be placed in a cloth sack. The neck of the sack must be securely tied. Fit a label to the sack stating exactly what is in the bag and your address. This is a precaution in case you should have an accident

Vipera lebetina (**Levantine Viper**). Under no circumstances should any beginning snake keeper attempt to maintain a venomous snake in his or her home. Too many keepers have died already from such foolish undertakings. ☛

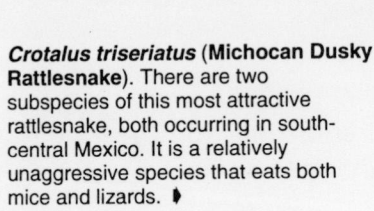

Crotalus triseriatus (**Michocan Dusky Rattlesnake**). There are two subspecies of this most attractive rattlesnake, both occurring in south-central Mexico. It is a relatively unaggressive species that eats both mice and lizards. ♦

Dendrelaphis punctulatus (**Common Bronzeback**). A resident of montane, bamboo, and rain forests, this slinky tree snake lays small clutches of eggs that already contain well-developed embryos. ☛

en route home. Police and strangers will know exactly what to expect. The sack can be placed in a box that also is appropriately labeled.

Quarantine

If snakes are purchased from different sources, isolate them from one another for at least 14 days. If all seems well, then they can be put together. A snake may appear well when purchased, yet be incubating a disease. This is true no matter how good the source from which you brought the animal. If later on you want to expand your hobby, each new addition must be quarantined before being introduced to your established stock.

Eryx sp. **(sand boa)**. A very widespread group, sand boas can be found in parts of Europe, Asia, and Africa. They are expert burrowers and generally are active during the early morning and early evening hours. ◄

Farancia erytrogramma **(Rainbow Snake)**. A creature of moist habitats, it seems to particularly enjoy cypress swamps. The Rainbow Snake feeds largely on eels and thus may be troublesome for the average keeper to maintain. ◄

Mixed Collections

The beginner should not attempt to house different species together. Do not house snakes with other herptiles (a collective name for both reptiles and amphibians.) Although mixed collections are seen on occasion, their keepers usually are very experienced. They know which species can safely be mixed. Safe is a relative term, though—there is always a risk, no matter how small, that a fight may break out.

Handling

The correct way to lift a snake is to gently but firmly pin down the head with a snake stick. Then grasp the snake securely about the neck just behind the head. This applies to small specimens up to about 46 cm (18 in). A non-aggressive specimen may be lifted at midbody. The snake normally will coil itself about your wrist and then can be rested on your free hand while the other hand maintains the grip on the neck. In some instances the snake simply can be allowed to move around as it requires, but within your control.

Farancia abacura **(Mud Snake)**. The only other species in its genus, Mud Snakes are particularly difficult captives because they seem to prefer eating amphiumas over all else. ◄

***Austrelaps superbus* (Australian Copperhead)**. Due to its highly toxic venom, this is a very dangerous snake. It rarely grows over 1.5 m/4.95 ft and lives in swamps where it feeds almost exclusively on frogs. ➤

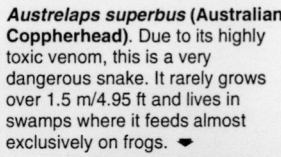

***Pareas margaritophorus* (White-spotted Slug Snake)**. A native of Southeast Asia (in monsoon and montane forests), it can be found in elevations as high as 1500 m/4950 ft and eats, as its name suggests, snails. ▶

***Dipsadoboa Aulica* (Royal Cat-Eyed Snake)**. A resident of South African riverine forests, this handsome egg-laying snake is rear-fanged and will bite without hesitation although it only rarely causes fatalities. It is also known as the Marbled Tree Snake. ➤

***Unechis nigrostriatus* (Black-striped Snake)**. Found only in Australia, it is in the same family as the cobras and kraits and therefore is unsuitable for captivity. The Black-striped Snake is active only at night and feeds entirely on lizards. ➤

A larger snake, up to 1.5 m (5 ft), should be pinned and then secured behind its head with one hand. The other hand lifts the body about halfway down its length. A snake any larger than this may need two people to lift it—one to secure it behind the neck and the other to lift the body.

Some snakes, including many large pythons and boas, become extremely easy to handle once they are accustomed to it. One rule must always be followed: never let a large constrictor throw a coil around your neck or arrange itself such that it can restrict the movement of your free arm! Careless hobbyists have been injured and even killed by incorrectly handling very large snakes.

If a snake is aggressive, the use of a grabstick (Pilstrom tongs for example) is recommended until the snake settles into its environment and is not so nervous. Gloves are not recommended because you lose the sense of touch. Additionally, you want the snake to become used to the feel of your hands and arms, not the gloves.

Bites

The bite of a small snake is unlikely to break your skin. Even if it does, it will be no more than a scratch. Swab the wound with an antiseptic and treat it as you would any other scratch.

A larger snake can inflict a deeper wound. In the case of large colubrids the feeling is somewhat like a number of pin pricks, followed by bleeding. It is later that the real pain and

Masticophis taeniatus taeniatus (**Desert Striped Whipsnake**). This snake can be found in the western United States and Mexico in a wide variety of habitats. ◆

swelling are felt if an infection results. Infected wounds must be treated by a doctor. The bites of large boas and pythons can result in severe lacerations followed by heavy bleeding and may require stitches. Remember that any deep bite from a snake is likely to become infected, so seek medical attention before a serious infection arises.

Arizona elegans eburnata (**Desert Glossy Snake**). Closely related to the genus *Pituophis*, the Glossy Snakes make fair pets. ◆

Astrotia stokesi (**Stokes's Sea Snake**). Occurring in waters from India to Australia, Stokes's Sea Snake feeds mainly on fish. It is an attractive animal, but its venom is much too potent for it to be kept in captivity. ◗

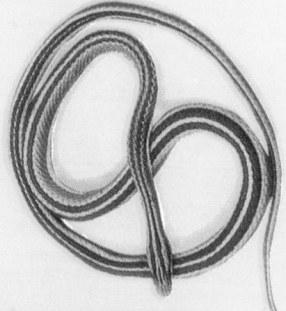

Psammophis leithi **(Pakistan Ribbon Snake)**. Keeping this snake in captivity is almost futile—the animal needs a great amount of room to move around in. It is also rear-fanged and somewhat aggressive. ☚

Amphiesma stolata **(Red Backed Garter Snake)**. A relative of the popular garter snakes, this handsome little resident of Sri Lanka, India, and Indo-China to southern China can be kept in a paludarium and fed goldfish ☚

Telescopus fallax **(False Cat Snake)**. The bite of this snake is thought to be quite harmful to humans, although actual deaths are unheard of. The False Cat Snake feeds mainly on lizards and requires very dry surroundings. ☚

Legal Obligations

A snake owner must determine what legal obligations exist. Federal and state laws restrict the keeping of certain species that are classified as endangered or threatened. There also may be local laws forbidding the keeping of any dangerous or venomous species without a permit. In this case there may be stringent insurance, housing, and security requirements. Many municipalities have another set of laws that may prohibit boas and pythons or restrict the number of snakes kept.

The snakes offered for sale in most pet shops do not require special permits as they typically are freely available non-venomous species. Even so, it is wise to check the regulations at every level. Legal obligations are periodically revised, sometimes in quite unpredictable ways.

Housing

The type of housing depends upon the species to be kept. For example, it is pointless to prepare a tall terrarium or vivarium out of wood if it is to house a ground-dwelling species from a humid or semi-aquatic environment. The wood will warp from the moisture and the snake will not use the extra "head space" anyway.

Once you have decided which species to keep, find out as much as possible about the area and country from which it came: the humidity, plants, average temperature range, etc. Does the snake live at ground level or in foliage? Take into account the eventual size of the snake or it may quickly outgrow its home. Armed with this information, decide whether to purchase a ready-made unit or build one of your own design. The considerations discussed in the following material apply to ready-made units.

Many pet shops carry an assortment of terrariums. This aspect of the hobby has advanced dramatically in recent years. These units are often complete with lighting, heating, and other accessories. They are tailor-made to suit the species to be accommodated. The drawback usually is one of cost. These units are not cheap, but the top models combine well-designed features with high quality materials.

Terrarium Types

Think about what the housing must achieve. It must allow for reasonable movement by the animal. The snake should be capable of extending a reasonable amount of its body,

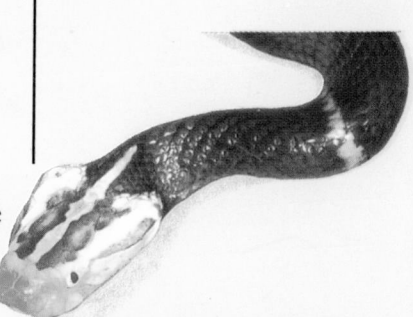

Azemiops feae (Fea's Viper). There are little data available on the captive care of this animal—no one has been able to keep one alive yet! It lives in cool mountain regions in Southern China. ◆

ideally its full length. It should be well built so it will be large enough to simulate a micro-habitat comparable to conditions in the wild. Also it must be secure so that the snake cannot escape.

A terrarium must be designed to allow ease of cleaning, and the design should permit you to get at the snake without difficulty. It should be long-lasting. Electrical fittings should be

Lampropeltis getula holbrooki (Speckled Kingsnake). A popular snake in the hobby, the Speckled Kingsnake occurs in any number of natural habitats, where it will feed on mice, lizards, and other snakes. ◆

13

incorporated neatly. Ventilation must be adequate.

Wood and Glass

Possibly the least expensive unit is made of wood and glass. This is suitable for species requiring dry conditions with low humidity (the wood will not warp). Wood of at least 6 mm (.24 in) is recommended. This should be given two coats of paint so that the unit can be wiped down easily although be sure the paint you use is not lead-based, as these types are harmful to snakes. The base is best made from timber 1.25 cm (.5 in) thick. The inner surface can be upgraded by covering it with a sheet of plexiglass or uncolored Formica®. The wood should be drilled on the sides or back

Elaphe obsoleta lindheimeri **(Texas Rat Snake).** This is a newborn example of a "leucistic" snake, meaning it has lost all normal pigmentation except for that in the eyes. ◄

Lampropeltis alterna **(Gray-banded Kingsnake).** One of the most popular snakes in the hobby—even though it can also be very expensive. ◄

with ventilation holes. Be sure they are too small for the snake to escape through, or cover them with metal mesh.

A circular or square hole should be cut in the roof of the terrarium and covered with strong, fine mesh. This provides additional ventilation, but its main function is to provide localized heat for basking when a heat lamp is suspended over it.

A glassed front viewing panel can be built into a hinged frame or it can be placed on runner so it can be slid open. The runners may be grooves simply cut into the wood, or they may be made of metal or plastic. The panel should slide halfway across the unit. The other half can be fixed or sliding, according to the size of the terrarium or your needs. Glass panels also can be made to slide up and down rather than across. Clear plexiglass panels can be used instead of glass and in many ways are superior to glass (they won't shatter, for example). This material is available in a variety of thicknesses. If glass is used, be sure that it is thick enough to stand up to a firm knock. Your glass dealer can advise you on the best glass for your purposes.

If the unit is not too long, lifting handles can

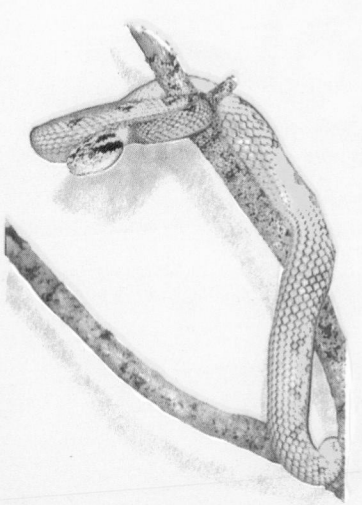

Bothrops aurifer (**Guatemalan Palm Viper**). This is a very lively and aggressive snake that will bite a human if given the opportunity. It likes to eat frogs but is willing to take other items as well. ▲

Erythrolamprus aesculapi (**Aesculapean False Coral Snake**). A remarkably pretty serpent, it occurs in South and Central America down to Argentina and has a remarkable resemblance to the Large Coral Snake, *Micrurus lemniscatus.* ◀

Loxocemus bicolor (**Neotropical Python**). An inveterate burrower, this snake can be found in relatively dry regions where it is active usually during the night hours. It feeds largely on rats and mice. ◀

be secured on the sides to facilitate transport. Be sure the handles are firm enough to resist breaking under the weight of the terrarium. In longer terrariums, it is useful to incorporate a sliding partition panel. The unit can be divided into two or more compartments to house snakes

Liotyphlops albirostris **(Central American Blind Snake)**. This is a snake not likely to be seen for sale anywhere. Ranging from Costa Rica to Paraguay, its diet consists mainly of very small invertebrates. ◄

Enulius sclateri **(Costa Rican Ground Snake)**. Snakes of this genus occur from southern Mexico down to Colombia. They like to burrow, seem active mostly at night, and rarely grow beyond 40 cm/16 in. ◄

Crotalus polystictus **(Lance-headed Rattlesnake)**. This was once thought to be an "aquatic rattlesnake" due to the large number of specimens found in swamplands. It has since been determined that this is untrue. ◄

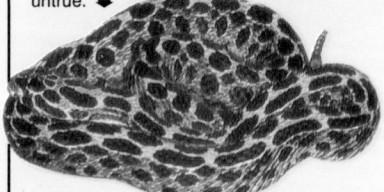

separately or allow easier access for cleaning.

Wood can be used purely to provide frames into which glass or clear plexiglass is fitted. This design provides all-around visibility. A frosted glass panel at the rear hides electrical wiring. Instead of using plain timber, plastic-coated chipboard can be used. Chipboard is more costly than plywood, but it is easier to keep clean. A sliding floor tray can be fitted to the terrarium to aid cleaning.

All-glass Terrariums

The development of silicone cements has been a great boon to aquarists and herpetologists, as they now can make their own units in all shapes and sizes. The angle-iron and putty tanks of yesterday were difficult to assemble. They were also less reliable when it came to preventing leaks. Nonetheless, for use as a dry terrarium, some real bargains can be found. Pet shops may sell old, used, or leaky tanks at discount prices.

If your build your own all-glass or plexiglass terrarium, look in your pet shop for a lid or top to complete the unit. This is particularly handy if you plan one of the more unusual shapes often seen today. These lids will have all the required electrical connections and could save you a lot of work.

Bear in mind that, when working with glass or acrylics, the larger the terrarium, the thicker the glass must be to withstand the stress. Once the accessories, substrate, water, and rocks are added, the weight of the unit increases dramatically. This weight also must be taken into account when placing the terrarium. The shelf or table must be strong enough to withstand the weight without bowing in the middle.

Generally speaking, aquarium-type terrariums are restricted to use with smaller species. Larger snakes are better housed in structures having glass fronts with the rest made of a more substantial material such as wood or cement.

Built-in Terrariums

One of the most aesthetically pleasing terrariums is the type built in to an alcove in your home. Here it is possible to have both the height and width needed. If sufficient space is available, you can use bricks to create superb backdrops. You could even create granite-like cliffs simply by cementing over rubble and broken bricks. Coloring agents can be used to create natural colors (again, be careful of the chemical makeup of these coloring agents). The backdrop should complement the species. For example, for desert effects, create a sandstone look to the rocks. A granite effect is better for species of more temperate or tropical climates.

In the case of potentially large boids and colubrids, this type of housing is the best you can provide, short of devoting a room to the snakes. If you opt for a large, built-in unit, think in terms of incorporating a good pool that has a drain system. Ventilation ports should be just above ground level as well as high up in the terrarium.

The more natural the terrarium looks, the more pleasing it tends to be, but this also means that there will be more potential difficulties in keeping it clean and smelling fresh. There must be a compromise between boring but hygienic housing, and more appealing natural arrangements that entail more effort in cleaning.

Masticophis flagellum (**Coachwhip**). Occasionally seen for sale in the pet trade, the one factor holding the Coachwhip back from greater popularity is its unbelievably nasty disposition. ◄

Telescopus beetzi (**Namib Tiger Snake**). Although this snake's bite has never been known to cause a human death, the fact that it is an aggressive creature makes it undesirable as a pet nevertheless. ◄

Coluber sp. (**racer**). Like the Coachwhips, genus *Masticophis*, racers also are notorious for nastiness and thus are avoided by most keepers. This is somewhat unfortunate, since many of them are very pretty and do fairly well in captivity. ▶

Candoia aspera (**Viper Boa**). One of the stouter members of the family Boidae, this animal gets its common name from its strong resemblance to the Northern Death Adder, *Acanthophis antarcticus*, and the fact that it has a fairly diamond-shaped head, which is a characteristic of the vipers. ☛

Lichanura trivirgata (**Rosy Boa**). Now here's a snake that has encountered a sudden burst of commercial popularity. Rosy Boas are captive-bred on a regular basis and they are usually quite affordable too. ☛

Drymarchon corais couperi (**Eastern Indigo Snake**). At one time this snake was common in the pet trade but today it is highly protected and can only be acquired along with a virtual tidal wave of governmental paperwork. ☛

Lighting

When purchasing lighting equipment, give some thought to the type of lighting found in the natural habitat. Species living in dense foliage or spend most of the daylight hours underground do not require as much light as those found in arid regions. Lighting has a secondary use, for lighting can generate heat. The extent of the rise in temperature depends on the sort of lighting used.

If lighting is the main source of heat, there is a drawback. In order to maintain the correct heat level, the lighting may have to be on for longer periods than is beneficial for the snake. In tropical zones there commonly are an even number of hours of day and night. Lighting should reflect this. Hence, it is better to keep lighting and heat as separate units, each fulfilling its own role. Furthermore, a snake always should be able to escape both light and heat at its convenience. Such an arrangement should be incorporated within the terrarium ecosystem. The most suitable form of lighting available today is a compromise between ultraviolet and white light.

Ultraviolet Light

One of the essential vitamins to a snake is D3. Its formation is induced by the ultraviolet rays of the sun. Normal fluorescent lights do not emit this, but special tubes have been developed in recent years that produce wavelengths in the ultraviolet range. They are available in various sizes and can be purchased or ordered at your local pet store.

It is known what beneficial properties such a light gives, as numerous species of reptiles are breeding or being kept in good health that before were difficult to keep. However, less information is available on the negative factors. It is unknown for what duration such lights should be used, at what distance from the animal, and at what intensity. A suggested time for use is six to 12 hours at a height of 30–38 cm (12–15 in) from the substrate of a small terrarium. In larger terrariums, larger tubes are needed or a bank of two or three at a higher distance from the substrate. Manufacturer recommendations should be followed, together with any specific information available from reptile societies and pet shops.

Crotaphopeltis hotamboeia (**Herald Snake**). A dweller of swamps and marshes, this snake is native to Central Africa and feeds mainly on frogs. ◄

Rhadinaea flavilata (**Pine Woods Snake**). A very small, very cryptic creature, the Pine Woods Snake occurs in disjunct populations along the southeast corner of the United States, most abundantly in Florida. ◄

Bothrops lateralis (Yellow-lipped Palm Viper). A native of Costa Rica, this handsome viper has very long fangs and a strong bite. The mothers are live-bearing and have litters that sometimes number in excess of 30. ◄

Snakes, and fictional creatures whose appearances have been inspired by them (like the one shown here), are often portrayed as cruel, savage beasts. Of course, snakes don't generally include children as part of their diet.

White Light

This encompasses normal fluorescent tubes, incandescent bulbs, spot lamps, mercury vapor, and halogen lamps. The latter two are suitable only for very large terrariums.

Since fluorescent lights give off a minimum of heat, these are preferred. Again, there are many models from which to choose. They differ in length and output. The intensity of light varies depending on how far the source is from the floor level, so even a high-output tube may not provide sufficient light at floor level if it is placed too far away from the snake. The lamp must be placed so that the snake can avoid it by retiring into the shadows or even into total darkness if it wishes.

There is evidence that prolonged exposure to bright light damages the eyesight of snakes—especially in crepuscular (those active at dawn and dusk) and nocturnal species. In such species, the ultraviolet light also should be used only in moderation until a deeper understanding of the correct photoperiod exposure evolves.

Photoperiod

It is useful to have the lighting controlled by a dimmer fitted into the circuit. This gradually reduces the intensity of the light so that the snake is not plunged suddenly into darkness. The addition of a dark blue night light of low wattage provides a more natural light to simulate the condition in the wild when moonlight would illuminate the sky. The dimmer can be set so that as the daylight tube goes off the blue light comes on.

As most reptile keepers seem to live in

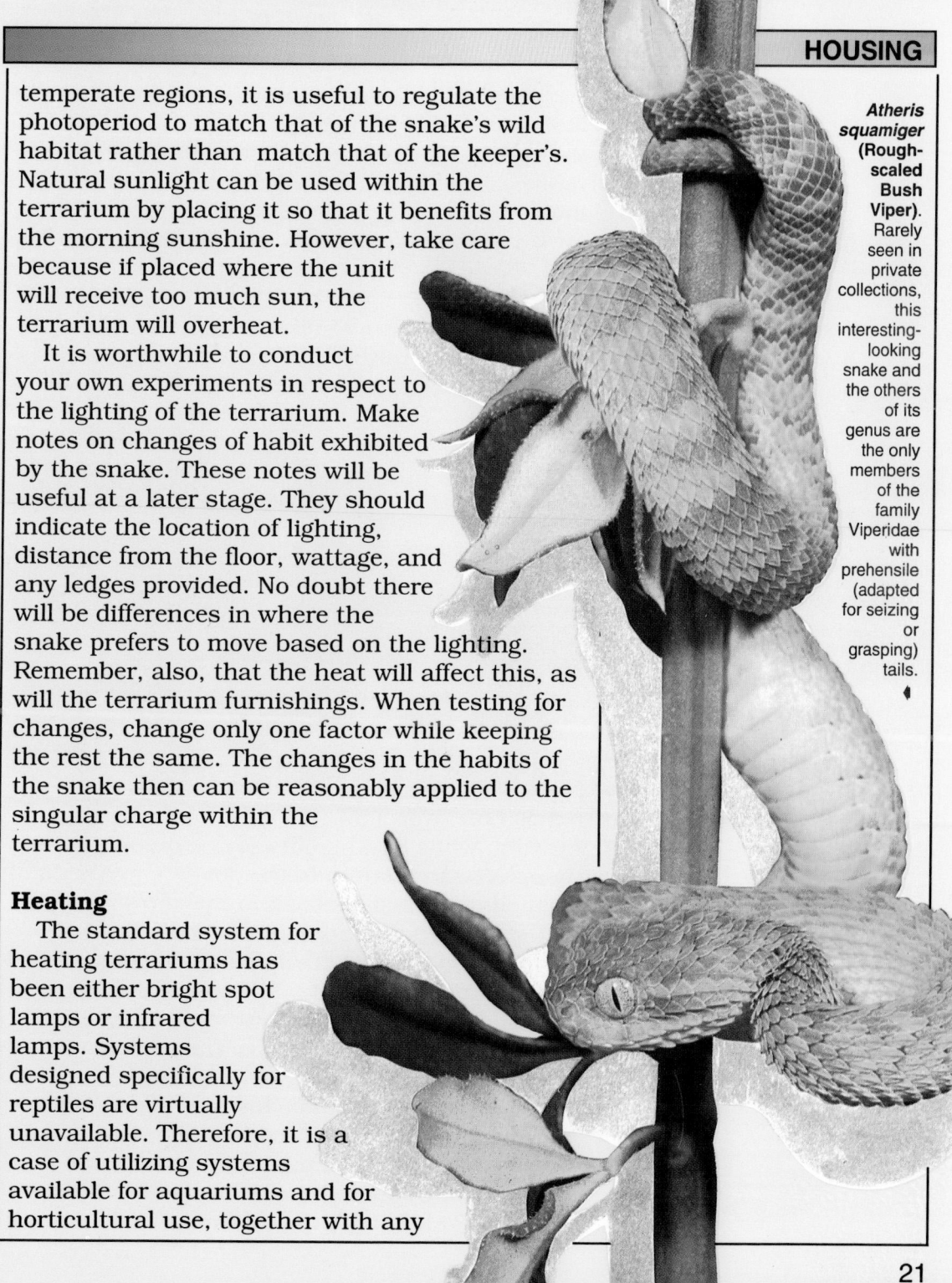

temperate regions, it is useful to regulate the photoperiod to match that of the snake's wild habitat rather than match that of the keeper's. Natural sunlight can be used within the terrarium by placing it so that it benefits from the morning sunshine. However, take care because if placed where the unit will receive too much sun, the terrarium will overheat.

It is worthwhile to conduct your own experiments in respect to the lighting of the terrarium. Make notes on changes of habit exhibited by the snake. These notes will be useful at a later stage. They should indicate the location of lighting, distance from the floor, wattage, and any ledges provided. No doubt there will be differences in where the snake prefers to move based on the lighting. Remember, also, that the heat will affect this, as will the terrarium furnishings. When testing for changes, change only one factor while keeping the rest the same. The changes in the habits of the snake then can be reasonably applied to the singular charge within the terrarium.

Heating

The standard system for heating terrariums has been either bright spot lamps or infrared lamps. Systems designed specifically for reptiles are virtually unavailable. Therefore, it is a case of utilizing systems available for aquariums and for horticultural use, together with any

Atheris squamiger (Rough-scaled Bush Viper). Rarely seen in private collections, this interesting-looking snake and the others of its genus are the only members of the family Viperidae with prehensile (adapted for seizing or grasping) tails.

supplemental innovations.

The type of heating must reflect the habitat of the species. There are a number of temperature ranges found in the wild. These may be divided into three broad groups, though in reality there are a number of gradients in each group.

Desert

The daytime temperature in this range may be very high, but it drops sharply after the sun goes down. There are many types of desert, and one

Lampropeltis getula "goini" (**Blotched Kingsnake**). Orange-reddish tinting is somewhat rare in this snake; the young specimen shown here is the product of carefully selected parents. *"Goini"* can be feed pinkie mice at this age. ✦

Oxyrhopus petolarius (**Forest Flame Snake**). A rear-fanged resident of the tropics of South and Central America, the Forest Flame Snake can cause irritating skin rashes and swellings. ➥

Oxybelis brevirostris (**Short-nosed Vine Snake**). These vine-like creatures (hence their common name) occasionally appear for sale in the pet trade, but most do poorly in captivity. Their main food seems to be lizards. ➥

Sonora semiannulata (**Ground Snake**). An inhabitant of many types of terrain, this snake occurs primarily in the southwestern United States and into Mexico. It feeds mainly on small invertebrates.

may not be the same as the other. In some regions the overnight temperature is close to freezing, while in others it may be quite high, though low in relation to the daytime figure. In such climates snakes bask in the sun to build up their internal temperature so they have sufficient muscular activity for the night's hunting and movements. This done, they bask again during the day, digesting their food caught the night before. The cycle is repeated.

A terrarium for this type of species should have localized heating with ceramic infrared lamps to provide basking areas. Strong spot lights can be used, positioned out of reach of the snake and covered with wire mesh. The snake might otherwise coil around the light and be burned. Underfloor heating can be provided by heating cables or pads produced for horticultural purposes. Remember that after the sun goes down the earth still retains warmth. The object is to simulate such a situation. Of course, the average terrarium is already in a protected and heated environment, so the overnight temperature may not drop that much. A bottom heater may not be required. Beyond those

Lampropeltis getula californiae **(California Kingsnake).** One of the most often sold and captive-bred of all snakes, the California Kingsnake makes a royal pet. It gladly will take mice (from your fingers), and most specimens have calm, controlled tempers. The example shown here is somewhat rare in that its vertebral stripe is unbroken. ◂

produced for gardeners, there also are undergravel heaters made for use by aquarists. Heater pads can be placed either below the terrarium or under the substrate.

Temperate

Many areas, such as Europe, much of the USA, and certain parts of Australia, have a climate that ranges between quite warm in summer to very cold in winter. The amount of light and heat varies considerably between the seasons. Snakes from these regions require local basking areas but cannot be kept as hot as the desert species, neither do they require as high a temperature overall. More humidity is required, though. A number of these species may exhibit short periods of hibernation corresponding to the coldest months of their region; this often

Crotalus tortugensis **(Tortuga Island Diamond Rattlesnake).** As with any rattlesnake, this species is best left to the fate of the wild and not kept in the home. Tortuga Island, incidentally, is located just off the coast of Baja California. ◂

Pelamis platurus (**Yellow-bellied Sea Snake**). It is rather unfortunate that this and other sea snakes are so attractive, because they are virtually impossible to maintain in captivity. ◄

Elaphe guttata guttata (**Corn Snake**). This animal represents what is possibly the most popular of all hobby snakes—the albino Corn Snake. Most specimens are both visually compelling and very amenable to the trials of captive life. ◄

Lampropeltis getula splendida (**Desert Kingsnake**). There currently are eight accepted species in the genus *Lampropeltis* and a great number of them are seen in the herpetological hobby. Some feed largely on other snakes and thus are more troublesome to maintain in captivity. ◗

Leptodeira nigrofasciata (**Black-banded Cat-eyed Snake**). Although the cat-eyed snakes are very attractive and only grow to an easily manageable 60 cm/24 in, the fact that they feed largely on frogs discourages many keepers from nurturing an interest in them. ◄

influences reproduction, hibernation being necessary to trigger the sex cells.

If the ambient room temperature in which the snake is kept is at a constant and suitable level, then no heating may be needed. This is one advantage of keeping species from a region similar in temperature to that in which you live. Humidity will be governed by the dual effects of ventilation and heat on water. The less air being circulated in a warm environment, the greater is the humidity in ratio to the amount of heat in that same volume of air. For temperate species ,the humidity created by the inclusion of the normal water dish is sufficient for most species. Slightly more water surface is needed where central heating is on continually, as this creates dry air.

Tropical

Some features of a tropical climate include less fluctuation in day and night temperatures and a much greater degree of humidity. However, snakes from higher altitudes of tropical regions benefit from a greater temperature variation between day and night. Even the day temperatures should be lower than those prevalent in tropical lowlands, river basins, and similar regions. This is certainly a case where knowledge of the animal and the area in which it is normally found is of great advantage. There may be drastic differences in temperatures from one area to another in regions considered tropical. Fortunately, many snakes are quite adaptable, especially if acquired at a young age.

Species from dense tropical rain forests are unlikely to spend much time basking in the sun. The ambient temperatures over a 24-hour period are constant enough to keep them in an active state. In such a terrarium the need is for an appropriate constant temperature rather than localized basking spots. The snakes still favor a warm spot when sleeping, though.

Rainforest snakes require a very high degree of humidity. This can create problems.

Producing high humidity is not a problem because, if the temperature and the amount of surface area of the water are correct and the air flow is restricted, the air will become humid. However, it will become stuffy, also. This increases the risk of disease spreading and can create smells.

A system should be developed where running water is passed through the terrarium. This way a good flow of fresh air passes through the housing. A small waterfall passing over rocks looks great and helps maintain high quality. The water can be recirculated via simple aquarium pumps and filters. Of course, the terrarium needs to be rather large.

Because there is a need for humidity, don't get the impression everything should be wet. A dry, warm area of substrate always should be available to a snake.

Echis carinatus **(Saw-scaled Viper).** Of all the snakes that should *never* be kept in captivity, this one tops the list. It is considered by many to be the most dangerous snake in the world. Its venom is extremely toxic, and the animal will not hesitate to use it if given the opportunity. ☛

Lampropeltis trianglum sinaloae x **albino** *Elaphe guttata guttata* **(Sinaloan Milk Snake x albino Corn Snake).** Hybridization has become something of a fad in the herpetological hobby. Most hybrid snakes seen for sale are uniquely attractive but some command a very high price. ☛

Pituophis catenifer annectans **(San Diego Gopher Snake).** Many "popular" snakes are now being bred in albino varieties. When new ones first appear they can be very expensive, but their prices progessively drop as their captive breeding increases. ☛

Thamnophis brachystoma **(Shorthead Garter Snake)**. There are many different species and subspecies of garter snakes but only a few of them are regularly seen in the pet trade. Garter snakes are lively, hardy, and inexpensive and are therefore recommended for beginners. ◄

Eryx colubrinus loveridgei **(Kenyan Sand Boa)**. Most of the sand boas are not seen in pet stores, so most hobbyists are unfamiliar with them. They are unusual in comparison to other boids in that they spend very little time off the ground. ◄

Thamnophis cyrtopsis **(Blackneck Garter Snake)**. A creature of varied habitats, it can often be found very far from any permanent water source. Litters are unusually small for *Thamnophis*—rarely over 25—and the adults grow to a relatively good size of 105 cm/42 in. ◄

Sturdy plants are an aid in producing a better tropical terrarium. They provide diffused lighting within the foliage, as is found in such regions. This may not be practical for extremely large boids, which quickly destroy foliage within the confines of a terrarium of the size the average hobbyist is likely to have. Another problem is bacterial and fungal spotting of plants kept in high humidities.

An even greater amount of water is needed in the rainforest terrarium. This can be heated using aquarium heaters controlled by thermostats. It is also possible to obtain heaters that operate in still air. These should be protected with mesh, as should those in water, so the snake can not be burned by them.

There are many possible ways to heat the air and provide the air currents in large terrariums. Bathroom wall heaters add warmth and small fans generate air movement. Fan heaters can be wired into thermostats, but they tend to be expensive to operate. Enthusiasts are constantly

◆ Elaphe guttata guttata **(Corn Snake).** Corn Snakes are excellent captives and can be fed entirely on mice. Since they are so widely bred they can obtained with very little financial output.

Elaphe obsoleta obsoleta **(Black Rat Snake).** One of the lesser-seen albino rat snake species, the Black Rat Snake often has the unpleasant combination of a short temper and a powerful bite. The specimen shown here is particularly attractive. ▶

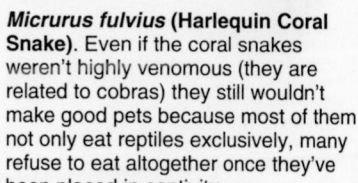

Eryx johni **(Brown Sand Boa).** It is perhaps unfortunate that the sand boas are not more available to hobbyists. Some species are very beautiful and most have a very gentle nature. ◆

Micrurus fulvius **(Harlequin Coral Snake).** Even if the coral snakes weren't highly venomous (they are related to cobras) they still wouldn't make good pets because most of them not only eat reptiles exclusively, many refuse to eat altogether once they've been placed in captivity. ◆

striving to arrive at optimum conditions in the absence of sophisticated equipment. It is worthwhile to visit zoos and specialist horticulturists who share the common problem of recreating ideal environments.

Terrarium Furnishings

Because snakes do not exhibit emotions as obviously as do some other animals , don't get the idea they are not subject to stress. This is not given enough consideration by some keepers. Most snakes are shy, retiring animals. When placed in stark, unnatural conditions, it is possible that gains made in hygiene are lost to stress. The potential longevity of a pet actually may be lowered in terrariums that are too clinical. (Many experienced keepers would disagree violently with this statement, however.)

The objective should be to arrive at an acceptable balance between extremes. For example, clean paper is more hygienic than garden soil. However, pebbles, gravel,

Thamnophis sirtalis sirtalis (**Eastern Garter Snake**). For most garter snakes, the tank setup needs to be in the true paludarium style—half land and half water. A large water bowl will often do as the water body, but the water will need to be changed often. ☙

Pituophis catenifer catenifer (**Pacific Gopher Snake**). This particular Gopher Snake can be seen in two pattern varieties—blotched and striped, the latter being shown here. ☙

Elaphe obsoleta quadrivittata (**Yellow Rat Snake**). Many keepers prefer to start with newborn captive-bred specimens (like the young one shown here). The main advantage is that these snakes have never been exposed to the wild and thus need no adjustment to captive living. ☙

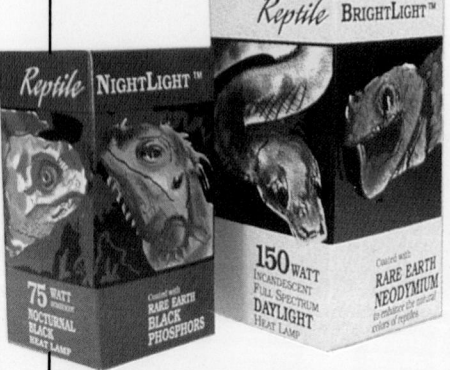

Pituophis catenifer affinis (**Sonoran Gopher Snake**). Anyone who decides to keep an adult *Pituophis* had better be aware that they literally are mouse-devouring machines. Five adult mice per week is not at all unusual for a healthy specimen. ▶

and aquarium stones are aesthetically more pleasing than paper while less prone to bacterial content than soil. These stones can be cleaned easily on a regular basis. By having an extra supply of stones, the supply can be rotated, one lot being used in the terrarium while the other is being cleaned.

Choose stones of a natural color. Buy various sizes, from very small to very large. A variety of peats and composts that can be used for substrate are available from your local garden center. The addition of dried leaves and twigs creates a woodland or forest floor look. Sand normally is not recommended because it can become lodged between the scales of a snake and cause sores.

Rocks can be arranged to give a natural look. They can be used to create caves, but do not position

Pituophis deppei deppei **(Mexican Pine Snake)**. Most *Pituophis* varieties are available to an interested person, but some, like this one, are very rare and will be very costly when they do show up for sale. ◄

Elaphe rufodorsata **(Chinese Garter Snake)**. A garter snake in the rat snake genus? Although the animal is technically classified as a rat snake, it has so many garter snake characteristics that its common name is inconsistent with those of the others in its genus. ◄

them in such a way that they might topple onto the snake. Rocks should be cleaned regularly. Again, have a few in reserve for use in rotation.

Rock formations can be made by covering lightweight plastic or wood with cement mixed with plasticizing and coloring agents. These are terrific in large terrariums since big boulders are too heavy to be practical.

Wood and cork are popular fterrarium. inclusions . Both can be purchased at pet shops. For climbing species, it is essential to keep a stock of suitable branches. These can be fixed into concrete bases. Even ground-dwelling species enjoy a certain amount of climbing.

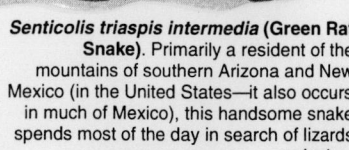

Senticolis triaspis intermedia **(Green Rat Snake)**. Primarily a resident of the mountains of southern Arizona and New Mexico (in the United States—it also occurs in much of Mexico), this handsome snake spends most of the day in search of lizards and mice.

If a mini-pond is included in the terrarium, an undergravel filter from your pet shop is useful to keep the water reasonably clean. A layer of gravel is required over this to assist the biological action of the filter. If the terrarium is a dry one, a larger water dish of earthenware or aluminum should be included. This is best sunk to its rim into the substrate to give esthetic appeal.

Dasypeltis inornata **(South African Egg-eating Snake)**. Some snakes subsist on a diet of nothing but eggs. Many of these are often birds' eggs, which the average keeper may have trouble providing on a regular basis. ◂

Python sp. **(python)**. Most of the pythons make good pets in the sense that they are very willing feeders. Young specimens are probably best because they require less food. Large adults can be very expensive to maintain. ◂

Trimeresurus sp. **(bamboo viper)**. Mice and rats are probably the most commonly utilized snake foods. Ambitious keepers can learn to breed their own. ◂

keep snakes, so conditions must be just right. Do not forget that plants, like snakes, have preferred temperature, lighting, and humidity requirements. The snakes and plants should have similar needs in these respects.

Plants are best potted. This way they can be rotated so as to spend a time in the terrarium followed by a period in a greenhouse. The pot can be concealed behind rocks or in the substrate. Cover the top of the pot with pebbles so the snake does not disturb the plant's roots. Where larger snakes are concerned, artificial plants may be the only option. Real plants are soon destroyed by large snakes kept in a confined environment. Artificial plants are best placed at the rear of the cage. They can be mixed with real plants to create natural-looking scenes.

Feeding

Nearly all snakes require a meat diet. This ranges from invertebrates in the case of small species to mammals, birds, and fishes in the larger species. A number of species will eat lizards, many will eat amphibians, while yet others will eat other snakes if given the opportunity.

Because snakes are fed whole-carcass diets, they normally do not need supplements. All of the nutritional essentials for healthy metabolism are contained in the carcass: protein, carbohydrates, fats, vitamins, minerals, and roughage from the fur or feathers.

Protein is necessary for growth and tissue replacement. Carbohydrates are required for muscular activity. Fats provide insulation and reserve energy supplies. Vitamins protect against disease, and minerals aid in the formation of good strong bones as well as assist in most metabolic processes. And, very importantly water must *always* be available.

Dead or Alive?

The feeding of live prey to snakes always has been a matter of bitter controversy. When snakes first appeared in the London Zoo , for example, they were very popular, but then the public realized that they were fed live ducks, rabbits, and other animals. Many influential persons protested. The matter was even raised in the British House of Commons. Reptile keepers argued that live food was essential, but the time came to prove them wrong. The London Zoo implemented a dead food policy. Live food was offered only where starvation threatened the life of the snake. The feeding of dead prey was found to be largely a matter of skill and patience. The keepers had to ensure that the snakes were in full activity and warm at feeding time.

Today the feeding of dead prey is virtually standard procedure with all zoos and hobbyists. Live animals may have to be fed when the situation demands it, as in cases of delicate, freshly imported wild species and of young snakes that initially may be difficult to convert to dead food. Few people object to feeding snakes live earthworms, insects, or even fish. The issue of live food is most debated in respect to mammals and birds.

Most snakes purchased from pet shops will accept dead prey. This can be gotten from pet shops, specialist suppliers, commercial poultry farms, and the like. The food can be bought in quantity and frozen. It must be carefully thawed to ensure that there are no frozen pieces remaining inside the dead animal.

The smaller the snake, the smaller the food item. Species such as the Smooth

Pliocercus elapoides **(Mexican Big-scaled False Coral Snake)**. One of many snakes mistaken for the venomous coral snakes, this one should be kept in a rainforest setup with a large water bowl. ◢

Liasis boa **(Ringed Python)**. One of the prettier boids, this species is not often seen for sale. It can be kept in a large, well-heated terrarium and fed mice and rats. ◢

Elaphe guttata guttata **(Corn Snake)**. Normally colored Corn Snakes may not be as popular as the striking albinos, but they are still very attractive, as you can see here. The Corn Snake primarily is a native of the southeastern United States. ◢

FEEDING

Your pet dealer has many good books about snakes and other reptiles.

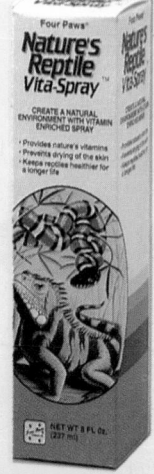

Nature's Reptile Vita-Spray by Four Paws was formulated by veterinarians and herpetologists and contains essential vitamins that are important for reptiles health.

A WARM CAVE The Repti Heat Cave from Zoo Med is designed to provide a secure, heated hiding place for all small lizards and snakes.

Green Snake, *Opheodrys vernalis*, subsist on a diet composed solely of crickets, locusts, and other invertebrates. A very large boid such as a Reticulated Python, *Python reticulatus*, needs much larger food, such as chickens, rabbits, and turkeys.

In the case of small snakes that are mainly invertebrate eaters, a dietary supplement may be required to ensure that sufficient levels of calcium and vitamin D3 are ingested. Vitamin supplements are available in pet shops. If no specific reptile vitamins are marketed in your area, try those developed for birds, not mammals. Because of variations in metabolism, reptiles and birds utilize a different type of vitamin D than do mammals.

Feeding Times

A small snake requires more regular feeding than does a large one. A general rule is that snakes up to 90 cm (3 ft) are fed twice per week, more if they are very small. Snakes up to 1.5 m (5 ft) are fed once per week. Longer snakes are fed once every two weeks.